# WHAT'S IN A TREE?

Tracy Nelson Maurer

Rourke
Educational Media

rourkeeducationalmedia.com

M000102632

www.rourkeeducationalmedia.com

Photo credits: Cover © James Steidl; Page 3 © James Steidl; Page 4 © 7yonov; Page 5 © Graham Taylor; Page 6 © frog-traveller; Page 7 © innocenT; Page 8 © Ronnie Howard; Page 9 © DDCoral; Page 10 © Stefan Petru Andronache; Page 11 © nikolaich; Page 12 © Tony Campbell; Page 13 © Jason Mintzer; Page 14 © Jonathan Brizendine; Page 15 © Steve Byland; Page 16 © Styve Reineck; Page 17 © Vinicius Tupinamba; Page 18 © LianeM; Page 19 © Nir Levy; Page 20 © Julie DeGuia; Page 21 © Eric Isselée, Xtremer, Hintau Aliaksei, Vishnevskiy Vasily; Page 22 © LianeM, Ronnie Howard, Jonathan Brizendine; Page 23 © Tony Campbell, Styve Reineck, frog-traveller

Editor: Jeanne Sturm

Cover and page design by Nicola Stratford, Blue Door Publishing

Library of Congress Cataloging-in-Publication Data

Maurer, Tracy, 1965-
 Tree : what's inside a-- / Tracy Nelson Maurer.
     p. cm.
 Includes bibliographical references and index.
 ISBN 978-1-61590-277-4 (hard cover) (alk. paper)
 ISBN 978-1-61590-516-4 (soft cover)
 ISBN 978-1-61741-137-3 (e-Book)
 1. Trees--Juvenile literature.  I. Title.
 SD376.M38 2010
 582.16--dc22
                            2009047304

Also Available as:
ROURKE'S
e-Books

Rourke Educational Media
Printed in the United States of America,
North Mankato, Minnesota

Rourke
Educational Media
rourkeeducationalmedia.com
customerservice@rourkeeducationalmedia.com • PO Box 643328 Vero Beach, Florida 32964

A tree is a busy place.

3

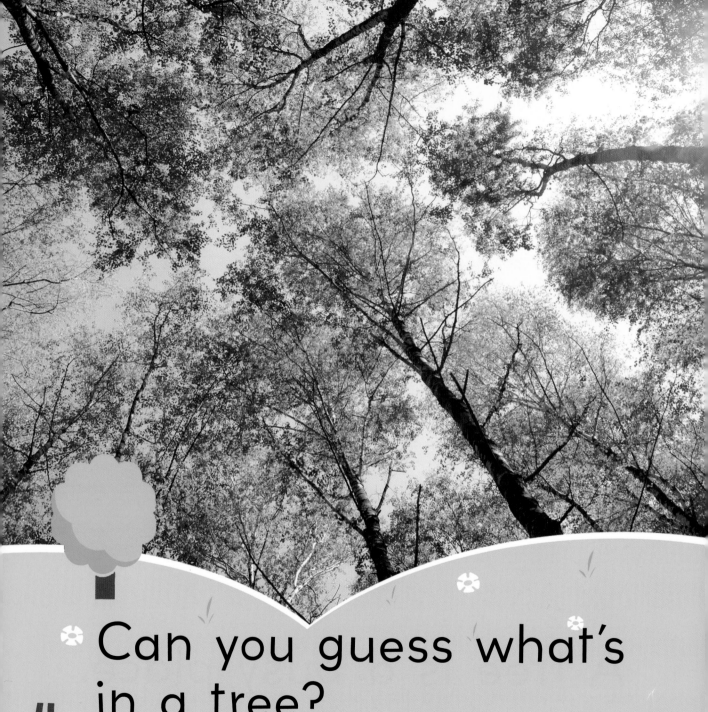

Can you guess what's in a tree?

4

tch tch tch

What eats in a tree?

A **squirrel.**

tweet tweet tweet

What sings in a tree?

A **bird.**

meow

meow

What plays in a tree?

A cat.

whoo

whoo

What hunts in a tree?

An **owl.**

ribbit  ribbit
ribbit

What hides in a tree?

A **frog.**

14

churr churr

What snuggles in a tree?

15

A **raccoon.**

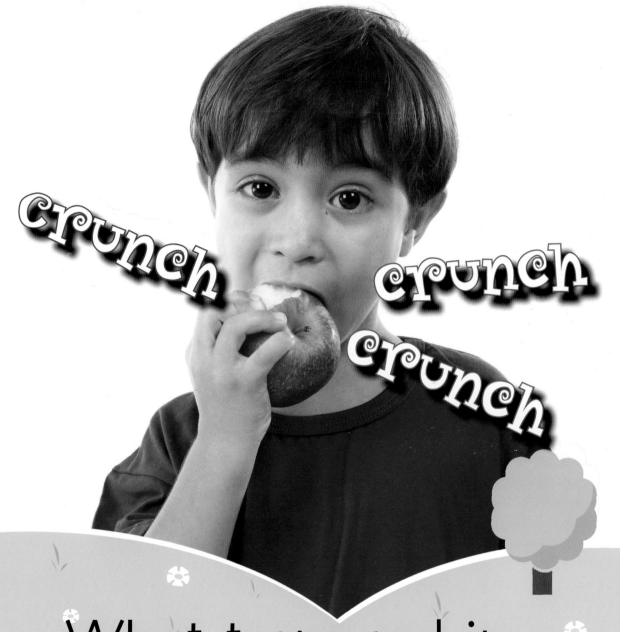

crunch crunch crunch

What turns red in a tree?

**Apples.**

whee! whee!

What swings in a tree?

# Me!

What else could *you* see in a tree?

# Picture Glossary

**apples** (AP-ulz): Apples are the fruit of the apple tree. Most apples turn red when ripe, but a few taste sweet when green.

**bird** (BERD): A bird, such as a cardinal, finch, or lark, may call out to attract a mate.

**frog** (FROG): A frog usually begins its life in water. Their green or brown skin helps them hide in the leaves or branches.

**owl** (OWL): The owl has large, round eyes to help see in the dark to hunt. Owls eat mice, rats, and other small animals.

**raccoon** (ra-KOON): A raccoon often makes its home in a hollow tree trunk.

**squirrel** (SKWER-ul): A squirrel gathers much of its food in the trees. A squirrel buries some of its food for the winter.

## Index

## Websites

www.kids.nationalgeographic.com

www.eol.org

www.inaturalist.org/taxa

## About The Author

Tracy Nelson Maurer likes to explore the area near Minneapolis, Minnesota, where she lives with her husband and two children. She holds an MFA in Writing for Children & Young Adults from Hamline University.

Meet The Author!
www.meetREMauthors.com